SLAVES OF ALGIERS

Kathleen Woolrich

01 JANVIER 2014

A series of photographs

Life becomes a series of photographs
And then we are not here anymore
If my heart can break
Then I am still here
If I can cry
Then my heart did not die

If I melt into the ground
Then it's only up from here
Life becomes a series of photographs
And then we are not here anymore
Love becomes a series of photographs
And then we dance across the photos
We bend and move
And recall the nights and days without sleeping
God has not abandoned me
But some days it feels like I am waiting for God
For days to start and nights to end
In perfect synchronicity
Love ends love begins
In perfect time
Up and down stairs
He might walk into a place I am
Or spin me around by my coat
Life is just a series of photographs

I'll wait for the moon

Sometimes you run against the wind
And race against the storms
And sometimes you swim with the current...
Just to survive its grip
Darling I'll wait for the moon
I know you are struggling
The moons smiles on you
Darling you are not lost upon the mountain
So many things will bring you home
I can't tell you the way I know
I just do
Keep your bonfire heart
And let it burn away the pain
Not everything will be a goodbye
So many things take so much time to unfold
Definitions of love and remembrance
Just look at the sky
Look at the night
And somewhere I'll look up at it too
And maybe our paths will cross
Jugurtha
Maybe some day I'll know more than the tracks of
your past
And help you see the moon shines for you
It shines for you too
Jugurtha

Did you think I would wait

Did you think I would wait?
Or grieve when you left?

Perhaps I do, and did and will
But my hair will be on a pillow as I did it
I will kiss the next one as hard as I can
And remember your weaknesses
Problems and faults
As I kiss him and listen to Ya Rayah
Did you think I would wait and eternally suffer?

Oh I do darling I do
But more that you know
As I make love to him
And remember your cruelty
I laugh at your faults through my tears through my
tears
Did you think I would wait build an altar and wait?

Perhaps I do, I do and will in my mind
But life is one of flames and passion even coated
with remembrance

Did you think I would wait?

Did you think I would wait?

The mountain in the room

You said when I left you
You never saw
Who I was till the room was empty
And my love not beside you
You said that you never expected the coldness
The loss and the pain
When I left you, when I left you
You said that you expected things to be different
My love is a mountain and adoring and eternal
But my nose is sharper and higher
That you will ever deserve
And I can love you and adore you
Yet refuse to return
And not ask Oualache... through my tears through
my tears
I swallowed the pain
And said goodbye to you
My happiness was worth more than loving you
And it was always the mountain in the room

Moonlight and asphalt

Moonlight and asphalt
And a thousand miles between us
And I cannot see the difference
Between aura and invisibility

You are on my mind and haunting me
Although it was so brief, so fleeting
The night was cold and your touch was warm
And I was so frightened I would not hear your voice
again

Yet you remained
As solid as the roads that line my city
Born in fire and paved with pressure
Nonsensical and unknown to others

The simplest touch and inner place
You shared with me, made me feel beloved
So there are a thousand miles between us
A million cars, asphalt corridors ahead of you
And behind you

But somehow I am with you in the moonlight
And you came and found me
And to this day, I really don't know how
We mixed this heady blend of moonlight and
asphalt... of night driving

And lost ways

But yet you found me

Somehow...
But I found me... when I left your side
My darling
Should I tell him that he's beautiful?
Should I tell him that even gone he did not make me
feel as if he was leaving?

Moonlight my darling

Think of me

And I am with you in the mountains of Setif and
always was
Waiting for your face and for you to come into my
life and show me

That what I thought were imperfections, were what
you wanted and needed

Moonlight

Asphalt

And a lonely place

Just you and me, Oumri

Just you and me

Justice took a bath

As we dove into the river
You didn't want to come
And I shouldn't have asked
And now I love you damn it
And you knew you were trouble
And yet you tried to warn me
But I wanted trouble like I needed oxygen

Justice took a bath

You were trying to save me
But I needed your brand of hurt
You wanted to save me from me from loving you
And you didn't want me to feel you
Or see you
Or have the windows opened
Or doors unlocked
You were just trying to save me

As justice took a bath

And we dove into the river

I had to paint it black

I cried and said I loved him so

As much as father son and Holy Ghost

He laughed and said I chattered so

I had to paint it black

I begged for life to take away

Everything that caused me pain

I had to turned the dials on the radio way down low

I had to paint it black

He mattered more than anything

To a witch, a ghoul a golden ring

to her and him the angels sing

I had to paint it black

I suffered so as patriarchs fled

and cherubs silenced

They all lay dead

And there was nothing worthy that could be said

I had to paint it black

I begged and turned the radio dials

I looked for him and all the while

He threw pearls to swine

And began to smile

I had to paint it black

In subtle protest I did close

The end of her, hail winters rose

There was nothing left, no words or prose

I had to paint it black

She led herself to the close of day

She knew her joy was led astray

As there was finally nothing left to say

I had to paint it black

If it makes you cry

If it makes you cry

It can possibly be real

You wish you could smack me

And I'll take it all back

Well you cannot

And I still can love

but you won't have access to whatever is left

I don't want to hear anything right on the surface

If it makes you cry I am in

If it makes me cry, I am in too

But if it's more of the same

without salt without pepper

Eat your eggs by yourself or with dumber people

Cause I like mine with salt and I like harissa

If it makes you cry, then it was worth it, it was
worthy and fair

Everything else was a waste of your time

I choose betrayal and tears over boring any day

If it makes you cry

If it makes you cry

The spell is broken

The spell is broken

The enchantment over

I won't love you anymore

You are not the hero I imagined

You are not the man I envisioned

And I am free from you

The prison

And the idea I had of you gone

The spell is broken

The enchantment over

I am not impressed or entertained

When I saw you I thought you hung the moon

Now nothing you do cannot cause pain

I was trapped inside each word you said

And believed that you were not mortal

The spell is over

Enchantment over

And I left in more ways than one

My fearless desire has left me

My fearless desire has left me

The brave tears and warm longing has left

That longing and safety

That my memories carried to me

I looked in a thousand faces to find him

I crossed my arms

And curled my legs beneath me

Wishing he would return

I would breathe life into dust

Hold on to a handful of nothing if he would return to me, if he would return

You are not him, you are mortal

And so am I... and I am sorry I placed a candle at your altar and roses at your feet

You hardly need them or want them and I step backwards

Head bent forward and shamed

No longer fearless and brave

Or adoring or strong

I could not face an audience of what I wanted to say

The shamelessness and fearlessness of my dress in
the closet

The audacity of love and I a prophetess of its power

Now hold it in a box and it will be buried

No longer given or willing

Only shamed and retracting

My valentine remains

Within my hands

As I walk across a frozen lake

To bury what's left of my pride

and my nose pointed down

will no longer face you

I cannot and I won't

The trauma too great

The fear is too strong

Jugurtha

A handful of nothing

what was I left with after love s bitter burn

a handful of nothing

and a dress in a closet

was it worth it, the pain that I endured and the nights I lost sleep

a handful of nothing

or rocks and dust in my hands

If hearts could hold things like hands

I would have cold water and sunlight

Rocks and whirlpools

and everything my mouth desired

what was I left after love s bitter burn

a handful of nothing

and a dress in a closet

Algeria you make me weep

Vast and uncontrolled

Scorching and freezing

Salty and barren and lush and accessible

You make me weep

You make me weep

I long for you

I dream of you

I can't find my way here without you

The pain is too great

I am just existing without you

You make me weep

You make me weep

You hold people I love tethered to your soil

Yet I cannot be with you or hold you or own you

I can only watch myself linger and suffer and drown

You make me weep when I remember how much I adore you

You make me scared when I know that perhaps you were the only one that loved me

Broken and twisting and complicated and futile

Algeria

Algeria

You make me weep

I take it all back

I take it all back

Every word, everything I showed you

Because i have to, because I have to

You have no time for idle praise

Or childish girls with silly dreams

I take it all back, every poem every thought every dream

You have no time to wander or walk with me

We ran out of time several years ago

This is simply a journey I must make alone

So I'll leave you to your grief

Because I can barely contain mine

A poets curse

a field of broken bottles and I laid it all out for all to see

I take it all back

I take it all back

Ill bury it instead

Instead of showing it or sharing it with anyone else

I take it all back

A ship upon the water

I am a ship upon the water

A frigate without a home

a storm without a landing spot

A windstorm without a rest

I am a ship upon the water

I have no port to call my home

I want to cry but I must stay strong

Through unknown currents and in dangerous ports

I am a ship upon the water

I am a ship upon the water

I dance in my sleep and when I wake

I cry myself awake and wipe my tears

And begin the dance of the day again until I wake
from slumber

I am a ship upon the water

Did I shake you

Did I shake you

Did we dance on paper

Did my passion awake the poet in you

we can find time for nonsense and discourse and
song

and bad wine and strong winds

and every heartbreak in between

Did I shake you, did I move you

Is there more of you there

I see a glimpse of the boy you were and I am still
here baby

Not knowing or guessing whether any of this makes
sense

Would you run would you fly would life move you to
tears?

Is there much of you left to lose?

I think there is and let's save him and wrap him and
hold him

I am no answer but I might be the question

Because I have much less than you

So let's dance and let's run and let's break glass around us

Let find common ground in the middle of pain

If I run would you look to see if I was anywhere close?

Or would you let me disappear with the knowledge I might have the key to unlock you?

The poet the writer the thinker my friend

Sometimes I am in sleep and cannot find shelter

I'm running but not towards you Jugurtha

Farther away let's pick flowers and settle our debts

I'll wait at the bottom and we will find our way out

When you are ready to climb i m ready....

Did I shake you, awake you... unsteady your feet

Is the poison your cure beloved..

Jugurtha

Love Sauvage

Some listen to books and need an instruction book

All I want is a love sauvage

To be devoured and adored in every possible way

Not analyzed and torn apart

Let me tell you the story of love sauvage

It's the man who will bathe you and put you to bed

If you are sick or weak but spread your hair across a
pillow

Because he adores you so

It's the feel of desire

It's the pouting and its consequences

It's the love you cannot stop but wish you could
control

That leads me into broken gated gardens

Some want the manuals the love stories and books

I prefer the pages torn and books tossed aside

I prefer a love sauvage spinning out of control

As I prefer waves rather than the safety of lakes

So here's to the women who want to hold on to the moon

A lover's embrace, words chosen and thrown

A love sauvage is all I desire

the rest of my dreams are mere mirrors or dead ended.

desire and pain hold hands in the end

I'll say good bye to good sense at every turn

the love sauvage is all we truly have left

after we have sold everything else to the world

My stormy boy

He's my stormy boy

And I'm his stormy girl

And I don't fit into his plans or on the side of his mountain

I don't fit on his sidewalks or streets

But if there was a cafe in Paris

he'd run right there to see me

to either sit outside and watch leaves blow

Or in a corner at night

He might let me see a tear

and I might cry too

But he does not have space for me

In his well-ordered life

But if there was a french cafe

And time was of no importance

He'd rush to meet me, down subway stairs

To Blanche or on Rue Republique

I know he'd find me, it's just the wrong place

Wrong time and his mind is just gone

Gone far away and maybe it's not

My stormy boy

My stormy friend

With this hand

with this hand

If I was a queen long ago,

I could hold a sword

I could order the fields around me burned

As the enemies approached

Sometimes when I dream

I dream I am Kahina

With my children gathered around

I know I must defend

I dream I am on a mountain side

In Algeria

And the fields are burning

I am telling the soldiers flee to the east, keep yourself safe.

I dream I am a berber queen, clothed and wrapped with rope

With swords on my hips

and in the fire

And I yell Tamazight

and I claim the fields below me

A queen

I see myself alone and cold

But knowing my people are safe

To be a queen to be a berber

To be Kahina of the Berbers

To be brave and tall and full of fury

To be a queen of the winter and who curses green
grass if it means substinence to the enemy

her story quieted as the arabs invaded

And washed her away, her bravery, her equality

and left her out of the book

that holds Algeria in its hands

Whatever is left over

Whatever is left over

I'll take and Ill adore

Because life slipped by and gave me people who hurt
me

and battered and drank and too my spirit

I once was called left overs by someone I loved

He told me as he left I was too old to be happy ... that
he took what he want

A passport, my time

So I'll take whatever's left over

Maybe a broken hearted man and we will hold hands
together

And together so broken, but joined might be healing

And we might not remain leftovers or lost things

So let's ride the trains that we never took

Let's look out the window and drive real fast

Let's drink the wine we never could afford

For life will pass by ever faster

Broken and battered... I still remain

In many ways the woman covering her head and begging for mercy

But as I run I escape the pain of the hurt

And look forward to days with leftover people

And together we can be whole and dance in the lightening

So here's an ode to all of us who life left behind

We buried someone we shouldn't have

Or lost in love again and again

We will build our own houses and our own rituals and be

not left over ones but whole and strong

I'll pick you up and you pick up me

and we can be whatever's left over together...

has been can be should be is with the right kind of love

And we will wash our clothes and our sins in a
common river

the lighter side of baggage is we have a lot to look
through

I'll take what you have and you take mine

We will find the best in both of us

And move on in some way

Our love through the cast offs will forever shine

In the world that we live

Whatever's left over

My heart in a box

If it were only so easy
I wish I could love without strings and barriers
I wish I could be anywhere but here

So here is my heart in a box
my precious friend keep me close
forgive me my trespasses and my crazy ways

as I float out to see on a fresh hell ride

So here is my heart in a box
Please do not bury it or throw me..

I'll stick around and if we can we can open our boxes
together

And talk about yes and no and everything in between

I give you my heart in a box

It should have been me

So many nights I was cold and cried

I asked for you to appear

To share my days and nights

And somehow I knew you were on your way

And arrived so imperfectly

With lightening flying from your fingertips

You crashed into my life

But then I held on to the wreckage

It should have been me

In your arms

It should have been me baby

I cry at night

Why wasn't it me?

Why didn't I get the chance?

To take your name?

I would have held it close to me and never let it go

Why did we have to meet after the wreckage?

When so little was left

Why did I have to hold your hand when it was
frozen?

And I spend all my time

Looking for cracks in the wall to let the sunshine in

And repairing the damage life did to you

And you finally felt relief, it was relief based in lies

And when you finally were set free, what exactly
were you set free too?

Freezing rain and winds and burned clothes and
broken things?

What have we been released to?

It should have been me baby

It should have been me

I should have been my smile you saw when you
escaped the hell you lived

And I hold your fragile heart

And I just understand

That tragically beautiful man I ended up with

was everything I really needed in the end

And I don t despair the walls and the darkness

And I haven t lost faith in him no matter how darkly
he speaks

I still see the child inside of him

Who daylight abandoned

And somehow he preferred abandonment to being
annoyed

Electric fingers and jagged edges

A Marlboro man

It should have been me

It should have been me

Atlas Was Burning

I wanted to love like the world was burning

Time was of no consequence

...

And the world was on fire

I tasted of him, mercurial man

Who chased regrets across time immortal

And had his own demons to tame

I wanted to love like Atlas was dancing

Holding my heart in his hand

And beckoning me

Taunting and teasing

As if almost possible

The night held more possibilities

As Bacchus would flow

Oh I did my darling

Love as Atlas was burning

And woke up fractured and frightened

But still very aware

That some of the best moments in life are the ones that are fleeting

And when we are burned by the fire of mercurial men

So raise a glass to the taste of mornings bitter burn

And raise a toast to the people who singe our soft skin

For they help us remember that we are still vibrant

And hold promise of love denied but ever alive

So here's a toast to the gypsies, the harlots and clowns

The lost and the ruse less, the mysterious and abandoned

For perhaps we are the Gods who dance across the sky

And leave stars as our path to beckon the night

So I call to the heavens

Darling are you still lost?

The gypsy

The narcissist

The rolling stone I once knew

I am safe in my bed while he wanders and travels

But I know the taste of that wandering too

The distance between day and night

I would love to tell you I do not understand

But I do my darling I do

I know the pain you carry

The ghorba is only a port

And the storms will carry us from land to sea and back again

The distance between day and night

In mere hours

I count them and wait each starfall

Each windstorm and each sunrise

And I count the days I missed with you

And the years and miles between us

Before life twisted you and then the black years did you in

That black decade with bloody triangles

and roadblocks

You lay behind walls and without a glimmer of hope

You held a radio instead of holding me

And no one came to save you

I died my own version of a death

But you struggled to breathe in the winds of Setif

And me on the ground, failing to breathe

The distance between day and night is far and wide

and light will always illuminate the path

The distance between you and I

is only far when I am awake

In slumber I lay beside you

In slumber you forgive me all the sins you put upon me

We dance at weddings in the mountains

We swim through grain and wade through streams

I came to find you and we left together...in sleet and snow

In storms and trauma

We remain without

the distance between day and night

The Disciple of Time

He was the harbinger

And he warned me that time was the enemy

It was the one thing we could not take back

Or get back

so I tried to infuse his life with music, with love and cover him

with all the sunsets and kisses he had missed

He was the disciple of time

And I was his pupil

Get angry he said

Because time had stolen us from each other

be bitter he said

Because we would never again see those days

And I would never again be lady Diana

And he the one who watched and waited for me from a window

He said be bitter be cautious

As I loved him without abandon

As I dragged him into the water

And pulled his pants from his body

And threw him into the ocean

I took him from the asphalt and led him into the ocean

And told him to taste every single thing he could taste

Salty water and bitter truth

And he fed me the poison that infused his blood

And I fought back

and told him time does not own us

You have to escape it like the rip tide

That almost took the children at the sea

Children who wandered too far out into the water

Like a rip tide, time is a natural master

You swim with it not against it or it will kill it

Along the shore as the currents try to pull you out to
sea

You swim horizontal to the shore darling

Letting it pull you means certain death

If you resist it like the rip tide, it will overtake you

But if you follow it and let it carry you, you can
escape its ravages, its pull its destruction

and you can escape the brutality of time, the
emptiness and the meaninglessness

I love you so disciple of time

It took me forever to be angry with time

And then time took over

And then I saw you and knew you were beautiful

And knew we were safe

And time was our master but it would not kill us

If we swam alongside of it and not against it

I buried my father and you were there

Telling me the truths all around me

Not realizing that I would be the one to lead the ones
who would not acknowledge me

That resistance could be futile

But it could be epic

I could stand alone against time, against pain,
against loss like the Spartans

I could drag you from the sadness that encompassed
you

And you and I disciple of time, could bury our
fathers

And make peace with our past

So I yelled at you, do what you have to do

But come home because I need you

Leave the clock at the road and remember when

Time stood still for both of us

Because when we are old and cannot walk

it won't be the busy moments we remember

It will be the times we did very little

And some might call me dumb or unrealistic or slow

But I find meaning in the meaningless

And love in the lost

So disciple of time, so bitter so hardened

I love you so... I won't let you go to be lost in the meager, the abandoned and the fields of regret

I shall come back for you so we can dance in the water again

And drink wine under the moon because we will not pass this way again

I won't let you wonder or be lost or forsaken

I treasure those 120 days, those minute those seconds

And while I am a student, I am not a slave to

The ministry of the disciple of time

I don't want to make a memory

I don't want to make a memory

Or wear flowers in my hair

If loving you is fleeting

Or if I am just a souvenir

I don't want to love with all my heart

Or throw my feelings into the wind

If loving you was just a moment in time

That I will never see again

You see I made all kinds of memories

With a man I loved more than life itself

I sold my blood and everything I owned

To give to him

And he threw me to the wolves

He took everything I offered him

And threw my love away

And when things went south in his small world

He looked for my hand to hold

You see I don't want to make a memory

If all I do is lose

I don't want to wear flowers in my hair

Or dream of better things

Those dreams will only bring me pain

And break my heart again

I don't want to dream of a better life

Or of holding hands until I am old

Or walking in darkened streets

Or smelling jasmine in the air

I'd rather know the ugly truth

Or drink bitter and cheap wine than sip merlot

I'd rather feel the cold and bitter wind

Than think warm winds belong to me

I'd rather know love is not in the cards

Than dream that things can change

Or lay in bed at night alone

Than know your touch could save me

I don't want to make a memory

If you will say goodbye

I don't want to love or give my heart

If in the end I will cry

I don't want to make a memory

I'd rather ache in pain

Of all the love I would ever have

Than know I loved in vain

For all those that loved and lost

For those of us who loved and lost
And jasmine's smell in midnight faded away in
photographs
And somehow things just did not turn out right

Here is my wish for you
May these broken roads you travel on
You never travel alone
When you pick up the pieces of your broken heart
just know that all was not lost

You tried, you danced and then you grieved
But you did not look at life out of the window
You saw life for what it could be and should be and
tried your best
For those of you that loved and lost
And grief became your friend

Know that one day somehow the roads will rise
And so will the moon above your shoulders
And you will understand
That treasures very well may await
For those that loved and lost

Burning ships upon the water
....Algiers

The burning ships upon the water
Algerian frigates, with pirates flags
And fire upon the deck
I am a pirate ship
Who sailed to places that most never see?
Yet is burning in the harbor
Burning bright
With timbers aflame
I am a frigate
Whose sails are etched with flames
And ropes turned into ashes
I sailed and took what I needed from life
Paying the price eventually
A pirate ship who never stole
But drank wine as the decks were lit aflame
I am a ship upon the water
A pirate ship, a frigate
Who has no port, perhaps Algiers?
If I can return as far her whitened walls
I am a ship upon the water

A little smear of ugly

Left a little smear of ugly

smeared upon my heart

left a little smear of hesitance

and my joy upon the pavement

I was innocent despite my years

And had never felt a twinge of malice

No one had taught me how to lie

Or walk across the barren land

That love and joy once owned

a little smear of ugly

remains across my heart

smeared with boredom, but could be fear

would be love but turned to spite

because love could never grow some place hard

and if you think its barren now

the softness still remains

like a scar or somewhere infected

the dirt remains

but the sorrow cannot grow

the ugly is but a souvenir

a damaged part, a bruised and bitter place

was what you left behind

an earnest kiss

a moonlit night

was what I left behind

I cracked your shell

And loved without reward

You left behind dirt

But I left you me

a smear of sweetness and unfulfilled desire

unrequited and beautiful

a ribbon across your chest

I left behind a piece of me

that you can never remove

You left me sorrow

but I planted roses

In that little smear of ugly

smeared across your heart

Darling does it shake you

Does it make you wonder

The depth of condition

The breadth of compassion

So undeserving yet so needed

The stanzas of bitterness won't set you free

But I did darling, I did

So now you bear it as if I wrote my name

Across your scar, across your scar

That ugly has turned to softness

Yes darling it did, yes darling it did

It burned as if pure melted metal

Or stitched itself with shaky hands

And held itself tight to blackened thread

And emptiness no longer remains

So ugly smear I see you still

On my white soft skin, that no one ruined

Despite their efforts, to turn it tough

And dirt is only dirt, it's less than mortal

But love is eternal and lives beyond the grave

For if someone loves you, you cannot shake its essence

Even if it's rejected or ignored or toyed with

It stands alone like a sentry in the night

A path to come home, a moonbeam a star

The fire within me, will burn off its remnants

After all soil can be removed

With tears or a bath

And the ugly smear will be washed away

And yet I remain with you, vibrant and silent

Static yet volatile

A smear, a song, the scent of a woman

by fire rejected, the dirt washed away

but love remains

smeared across your heart.

Walking in the center

So many things I want to say to you
I love you
why did you leave?

What could I have done more than I did?
I miss you
And I am walking in the center
In the center of my soul
Missing every part of you
Wishing you were with me to help me mourn our
son
Wishing you were strong enough to see how much I
loved you
And all the things in my limited capacity that I
wanted to give you
I tried harder with you than I ever tried with anyone
in my life
To love and nuture, to caretake and to adore
But sometimes the shell we inhabit is not beautiful
enough or young enough
And sometimes we make mistakes
And I have had to say goodbye to you and a year ago
our son
And I love you more today than I did yesterday
And I want to know how deep my love can go and
where it can carry men
Is it possible to carry a lifelong torch for someone?
Is it possible to not say goodbye even though the
other person has?
I think its walking in the center
Walking in circles demanding love and loyalty that

another person does not possess
Or forgiving when you yourself are not forgiven for
any infraction
I am walking in the center
I should say I am walking in circles
Wondering why you mistreated me
Why you abandoned me without reason
Why you held me up to impossible standards that I
never could meet , only to switch the standards
My son is gone from me and I cannot say goodbye to
him without you
On the one year anniversary of him leaving us
I love you still
Although you yourself told me that if someone loves
you , they make sacrifices
Ones you were unwilling to make
So I will make what's left of us bloom
I will place flowers on his grave
I will treasure your memory
Because I love you
Because I know perhaps the pain of losing him was
easier transferred to me
And that maybe you need a new chance, to love and
grow and change
I adore you, I forgive you, I love you
That's the question I asked myself
How much did I love you?
I loved you enough to understand that maybe
leaving me was what you needed to do to forget
about our baby
And that maybe like I visit him, I visit you and me
when I visit the cemetery
Because all my love lies there and you were part of

him
My beloved

The keeper of the flame

I know now who holds the flame
I looked for it in the eyes of others
It lies in the eyes of the romantics
The fire lies in the eyes of those who value true love
above all
Hopeless romantics hold the flames
Those of us who look for happy endings and slip
hope into darkened rooms
I know who holds the flame
The ones who hold the flame are those that know
that love endures past broken hearts
It endures past situations and the continuum of time
It endures past love and loves losses
It endures anywhere that someone continues to
honor and long for love
For devotion, in a soldiers heart who lays on a field,
who died for country
In endures in a mothers heart who buried a child
In endures in a lovers heart, who was left alone and
longing for someone who is no longer there
I know who holds the flame

What do you see when you see me?

What you see

What do you see when you see me?

Do you see a dishelved 46 year old?

I have born 4 children, one not here

Three are here, one is grown and is a happy woman

One is a teenager getting ready to fly

And one is 8 and loves the wizard of Oz

What do you see when you see me?

Do I seem less than perfect? Or maybe past my time?

I struggle to walk as my bones burn and ache

I take medicines to breathe because water fills my lungs

And maybe I don't arrive to you in the most amazing package

But my heart dances, it does

I speak several languages and I have danced in the

Sahara

I have stood on Ireland s shores

And felt Swedens bite

I have stood in the middle eastern air

And lived a full life

So I tell you this

When you see the packages that arrive in front of you

When you meet a person who does not exactly
connect with you

Look beyond how they arrived and learn from their
journey

Grief may cover their face

But underneath the package may lie the answer to
your life

Or mask a friend who will be the one to save you

Because we do not always look like the queens or
kings we are

Thank you to the people that love me in this package

Worn along the edges

That love my words or the fact I always ask question

I treasure everyone who has walked with me

And yes I might be slower

Or older

Or fatter than you want to be with

But I have lived a full life and I will treasure you

My beloved friends

My compatriots

As we journey on this crazy long and winding road

Together, maybe disheveled , maybe broken

But always yearning, for one more happy day and
one more second chance

To be the Queens and Kings we were born to be

If I was beautiful

If I was beautiful
You would see who I was
You would hold my hand and dance with me and
honor me and love me
If I was beautiful
You would have wanted to dance with me, to walk
with me, to hold me
Maybe you would not have left
If I was beautiful
I would have had the happy ending, with the child in
my arms that we created
You would have seen when I gave every last thing I
had to make you happy
You would have appreciated everything I went
without to make sure you were happy
Every hair cut I never gave myself
Every dress I never bought
Every debt I incurred
Every mile I walked not knowing if I could walk the
whole way
If I was beautiful
If I was beautiful

A Rhapsody in Black

a rhapsody

a song

composed in black composed in slumber

if I could stay asleep till he returns

I would be the better woman

Only I know that I lie between the pages of a book

with wings flailing

trying to lift myself off of it

he does not know

that though I look like the stronger one

the straw that broke the camels back

perhaps was not the one anyone thought

a choice, a word, a poem, a phrase

hungry for the affirmation

I lay in bed in tumbling slumber

and moved to the couch

and tossed in fear

the love was strong enough to do me in

where others could not reach me

He did, my darling did

He only sees the stronger side

My broad strong shoulders to burden the truth

But my love for him is a rhapsody in black

in shadows and in longing, in fears and in betrayal

He cannot see my armor is pierced

with arrows carelessly launched

And an audience of one

Since only I know

The depths of my love for him

So if I am silent and melt into the bed

And do not awaken, will anyone notice?

Will the world spin without me?

Perhaps

Perhaps the wind will blow and life will go on

And my rhapsody in black

Be a song barely sung.

Maybe whispered and silently a durge will play

If love was enough

I would win the fight

If love was enough to win

But I was the lesser one, the more broken one with
more things than I could hold

The weaker one

Who sang brightly and clear?

But sank into the night

Perhaps slumber will save me, perhaps not

I was only the queen when he made me so

If my crown was pulled off, perhaps it won't be given
again

Perhaps I lost already and no one told me

I love him so, the winds please listen

I love him so, the winds please hear me

The water the lake the rivers who run

Tell them I love him so he can hear me

As I cry for him quietly for him to return

The blackest song plays as I lay in the darkness

The blackest song cannot give me rest for the weary

I love him, my winds that circle his feet

And that face his back with the heat and his memories

Tell the dust storms I adore him and miss him I do

As I lay alone dancing to the rhapsody in black

Become one of the ghosts

When I close my eyes

You become one of the ghosts

Beautiful and intelligent

But simply made of thin air

you curse my breath and name

and yet I never was the one to cut your skin

or break your back or make the scars

yet you rain hell down on me for the smallest thing

Become one of the ghosts I say

That's what you deserve

If you want to float and wander and take and hurt

Ill close my eyes and you disappear

Become one of the ghosts

And never face my questions

You want silence? You got it. I have rooms of it to
lend you
I have silence for years and days and months

You can walk in any one of the rooms and sit in the middle of it

I am simply not mad but I won't wear a dress

That I did not sew and clean a mess I did not make

So become one of the ghosts

And haunt yourself if you must.

It's what you might need

Become one of the ghosts who haunts my brain and my heart

I'll see you at night and hear your sweet voice

But to curse me, oh no you won't

Queens won't allow

So become one of the ghosts with your guitar and your smile

And I'll lock you away in my memory

Become one of the ghosts with your song and your stride

Just become one of the ghosts

Become one of the ghosts

Le Vent Boheme

You pay a high price to be a gypsy

the winds blow fierce and dryly

there is no rest for a gypsy soul

there is only understanding as the gypsy's feet hit the floor

and begins to run as gypsy's often do

Is it freedom that names the gypsies life

For I am a gypsy with ties that bind

I might have every reason not to run

Or miss the wind or the open road

the gypsy girl doesn't have the freedom a gypsy man might have

But she has the wanderlust and the thirst for abandon

for blood to be spilled with temper or tantrum

or love to be made under a star lit sky

I stopped my soul mate from breaking what he loved so much

and it was as if he longed to crush and destroy

that which he treasured to prove he was unworthy

I told him that cyphers that reminded him were less than he deserved

He needed to be challenged not catered to not ignored

He needed the safety of resistance a challenge

He wants no resistance to his gypsy ways

But I won't let him forget he is a king of his own

La Vent Boheme is what he seeks

He wants the easy answers, the passive and unaccountable

but a queen has to stand for protection and take decision

Not leave the gypsy to struggle without direction

Is she a bitch or a queen or a mother or both

A wolf, a tiger and the wind faces her back

She stands like a sentinel upon the mountains

And loves him without abandon without error or trial

the night is a mistress for my gypsy king

the road is his mistress but I'll watch the road ahead of him

like a queen guards her king when he's facing dark knights

the vent boheme will always be a stronger wind than the fragile will stand

It reeks of death and goodbye, it smells and tastes like regret

his glasses are full of regret and bitter wine but there is beauty up ahead if he would just take the chance

to trust himself and forgive his misspent youth

And to realize that perhaps the gypsy wind is perhaps not in him but all around him and will warm his way home, where ever he will go

Gypsy man can't you see that you were not ever truly lonely

that love lived inside the ugly truth you clung to

as a reason for leaving for living or dying

that love surrounds you wanderer and floats upon
the dusty currents you want to own

The currents of La Vent Boheme

A handful of nothing

what was I left with after love s bitter burn

a handful of nothing

and a dress in a closet

was it worth it, the pain that I endured and the nights I lost sleep

a handful of nothing

or rocks and dust in my hands

If hearts could hold things like hands

I would have cold water and sunlight

Rocks and whirlpools

and every thing my mouth desired

what was I left after love s bitter burn

a handful of nothing

and a dress in a closet

To come back

I am not strong enough

To come back

I am not strong enough

to even be fractured

or tossed and turned by indifference

Take it

here is everything I wrote upon the ground

here is every piece of paper, every word

I cannot hold it

I cant hold up one side of shroud

Ill let it drop to the body of where you used to be

When hope and love was your friend
I will not wash it I will not hold it

Your shroud is simply yours and yours alone

I cannot come find you

Only you are the one who can find me

To break that spell of thinking no one will ever know

so here are papers scattered on the floor..

I have to run.. I have to leave

my bonfire heart will rage alone

and candles flame

the whole night through

some trains you miss

some songs unsung

and some clutch their burial shroud rather than lay
it down

It wasn't in the cards

If I was not a priority

I sure won't be an after thought

I ll go out blazing and broken

It wasn't in the cards

I don't need an audience

To share my thoughts with the moon

It was always just the moon and I

I want nothing more

No other chance

No other thought

And no other song

It wasn't in the cards

And it won't be something that I will look to find

Red is the rose

My safety is in my sacredness and silence

If I can't have a thought between me and the moon

Then I don't want it at all

The stars are not allowed to hear my heart

Only the moon

It wasn't in the cars

And I cannot cross your path

Id rather be on the lips of a fool

than under the shoe of a brighter man

It wasn't in the cards

It wasn't in the cards

Let's write some nonsense

Let's write some nonsense

Cause we can cause we can

let's mess up syntax

Spell like gangsters

Because there is too much time to lose

Lets write some bad poetry baby

sweet and nonsensical

nasty and wretched

and lets love like it's going out of style

You can have a warning label and I just might not
read it

let's just break all the plates and glasses and give up
on rules

OK Maybe I will walk a straight line but not this time
baby... not this time

because there is no incentive to behave

Lets write some bad poetry

and make up stuff as we go

Lets write some nonsense, you and I

Lounes

Some curse the day you became too brave

That your life would have been better suited to remain with us

To dance to the sounds of Tizi Ouzou

and hold a teenagers pen to push him to write

But Lounes dear Lounes

You knew best

A berber spring would come again and you would be there with your beloved

You are with us in the mountains

when a child is born and speaks his first word

You are with us when a promise is broken

Or we forget what bravery is

Lounes

Some curse your name for going home

And say why did you do it

Why did you go

To fail and die a heroes death

but perhaps you knew that love is bigger than
murder

and that you would be a berber flag

ya boualem

ya Lounes

Tahar

Farewell my poet

My writer

We shall not weep

For all that is gone is your flesh and blood

Your body lays abandoned

But we will come take you

Our son

To wash and bury and take you to heaven

Our writer our son

You asked too many questions

But died with the answers

Across your face and hands bound

Our tahar our earth

Our son and our heaven

Our darling child of the fields

We mourn you

The Base of the House

With this stone

I send you back my darling my darling

You have come but the wolf is at the door

I'll make you strong Lounes

I'll make you strong

And you will remember the man I married is you

Now war is upon us

And the wolf is at the door

Go back and save our honor

For there are no more days to waste

If you come home and they enslave us

Then we might as well have lost our life

I am the base of the floor of this house

I am your wife

Now turn on your heels and return to battle

And call my name when you have won

My king my king return to battle

I'll be a ghost

If I share my basket

and open up my heart and life

and you don't find me worthy

don't look inside and don't inquire

I'll walk like a ghost right past you

and never turn around

those things I carry are all I have

my strength is very minimal

I have very little left

so it's not what you want

and you can't see its value

let me be a ghost on the walls

walking by in the night

I won't try to convince you

Ill simply escape you

And make sure I don't suffer from any more ills

I'll be a ghost in the garden

It's as if I never walked by

Or made a shadow on the ground

I'll be a ghost

I'll be a ghost

I'll be a ghost

Kathleen Voss Woolrich
2125 Shaffer Place orlando florida 32806

ISBN: 978-0-578-13858-9

www.ingramcontent.com/pod-product-compliance
Lightning Source LLC
Chambersburg PA
CBHW022030090426

42739CB00006BA/357